For Caitlin,
who watered

ISBN: 978-0-9941799-1-3

Publication year:	2015
Book Title:	Poet Tree Book
Language:	English
Publisher:	Michael Raymond Astle
Printer:	Ingram Spark
Location:	Melbourne, Australia
Author:	Jessy Carlisle
Illustrator:	Terri Kelleher
Binding:	Hardback
Target Audience:	Family
Subjects:	POE003000 Poetry: Inspirational & Religious
	POE010000 Poetry: Australian & Oceanian
	POE000000 Poetry: General

A Tree's Lament

I, am a tree.
A tree of old.
I stand atop a mighty hill.
I have seen war;
I have seen death;
I have seen both famine and plague.
I, have been afflicted.

Yet do I stand and live.
I alone survived the hewers,
The droughts and floods
Of times gone by.
Now I gaze in splendour o'er lands
Without a tree.
I am, a tree.

A Mystery

Throughly in the forest green
Search I for a beast unseen
And though his plosive power be
Much greater than the strength of me
'Tis his size which gives me hope
He is small that I may cope
And there amongst the bushy trees
I find him hidden in the leaves
So he may not live much longer
For now 'tis I who is stronger

Garden Window

Inspired by Heather Window's
acrylic artwork "Floral Escapade"

Through the petals, o'er the leaves
The Master comes to paint the trees
Where the pixies dance and gaze
As air's fine mist clears new dawn's haze.
For when the dew flies back home
'Tis then cold earth claims ev'ry gnome!
So vibrant flowers may greet you,
Yet they must obey their curfew
Lest the Master make them die
'Fore they exalt themselves too high.

Butterfly Song

The Butterfly, the butterfly
He flaps his wings and
Flutters by
New name for an old being,
Oh how you were...
Just a little egg

Caterpillar hatch your egg,
Go and eat some leaves instead
Climb the trees
Chew as you please
In the winter don't you freeze.
Go build up your own cocoon
Caterpillar winter's soon
You will hide away from moon
As change makes your wings

Cocoon stay hidden from the winds,
Birds and worms and other things
Winter's tomb is made in May,
But he breaks another day
Little bug you sleep to grow
'Til in spring you say 'hello'
So come and bring us love

Though your life is very short
Butterfly you teach us ought
So we may now go and think
How in life we should take win's
O thank you butterfly
O thank you God for him

Water is Grand

Rain fall gently from the sky
Though one may wonder why.
You fall upon all the earth
That she may again give birth
To another sweet fruiting flow'r.
Yet from whence be thy great power?
One young droplet or a torrent strong,
So soothing a sip or a drowning throng ~
Such virtues are magnificent!
Will thy strength ever be all spent?
Perfectly harnessed in form!
Each part both king and a pawn
Acting always as one,
'Til all be o'er and done.

Friend of Darkness

Black cloud in the sky
Sent to water, purify
Hard and dark you may appear
But I know why you're really here
You're only sent to bless the land
You're just here to lend a hand
Though so many speak your ill
My lips love you still

Days of Thunder

Days of thunder,
Nights of rain,
Makes one wonder,
Why this pain?

Torn asunder,
One now twain,
Did I blunder?
Did you feign?

Why to this darkness
Must our light wane,
When for the heartless
You wear this chain?

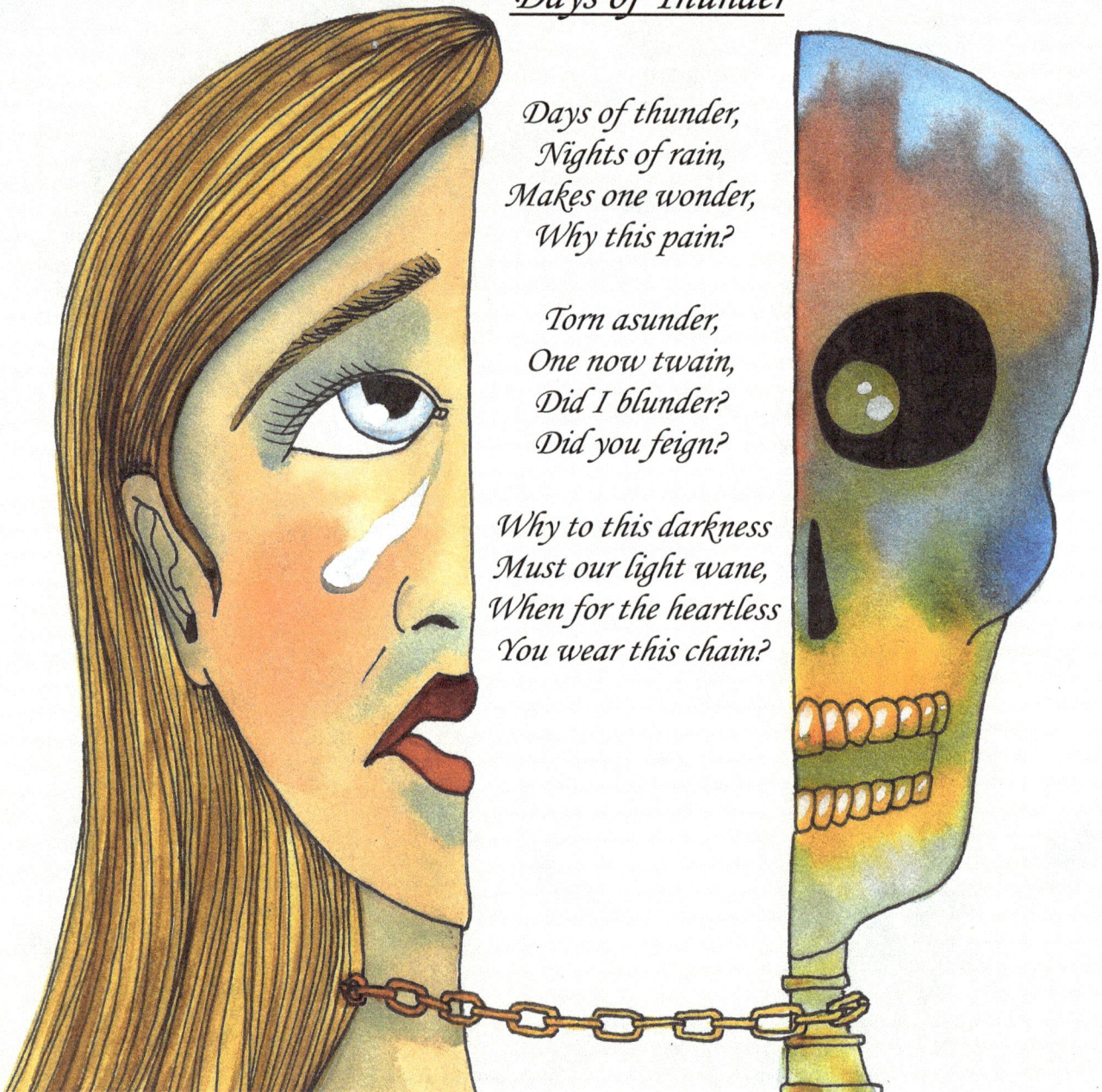

Hear the Youth Call

Oh how I long for the days of my youth
When all was well and happy.
When I could wake and sleep at pleasant times~
Until the world called to me.
"Come, follow us; be not fulfilled or saved."
I try to speak to the world,
"Why do you blindly approach death, O world?"
Yet the world keeps on calling,
"You man, mighty and brave, follow our way."

"Look at your troubles, O world.
How is it you claim your way to be right?"
Deafly the world marches on.
"Forget the good things, embrace the world's way."
"Oh world, when will you hear the
One young voice, crying, in the wilderness?"

Ode to Knightsbridge

My street is the Himalayas
As turbulent as a snowstorm
Where the heavens meet the forests
As new spring's warm sun kisses green
tree tops

There high hills roll strong as thunder
As all beasts meet, civil and wild
Where old knights guard her pillars firm
Yet the feet of Everest are silent.

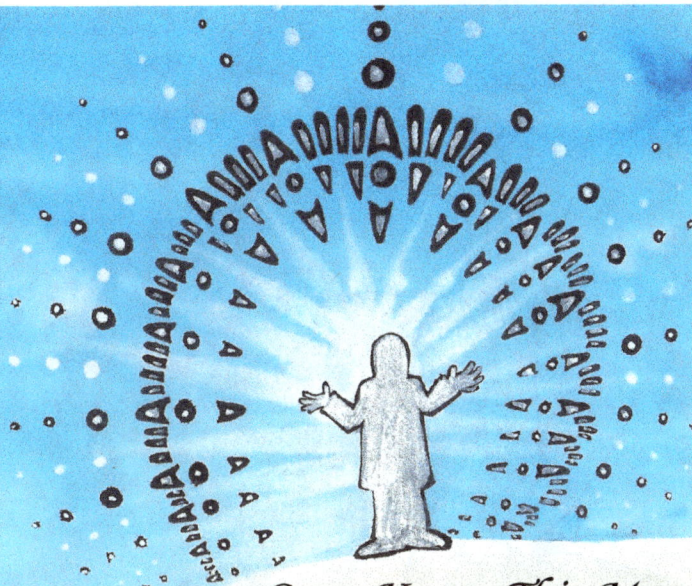

Come Know This Man

Who is this man who yonder stands alone?
He seems quite close as though I might have known
Another man with glory such as he.
Who is this   man and how can this be?
I have never   once seen this stunning man
And yet somehow   I know that I once ran
Alone with   this man up my greatest hill.
But now   in the silence, we both stand still

And I wonder if I should go to him.
How could I compare to his glowing rim?
As he drifts off behind the hill I cry.
He's wondrous, and yet often shunned, but why?

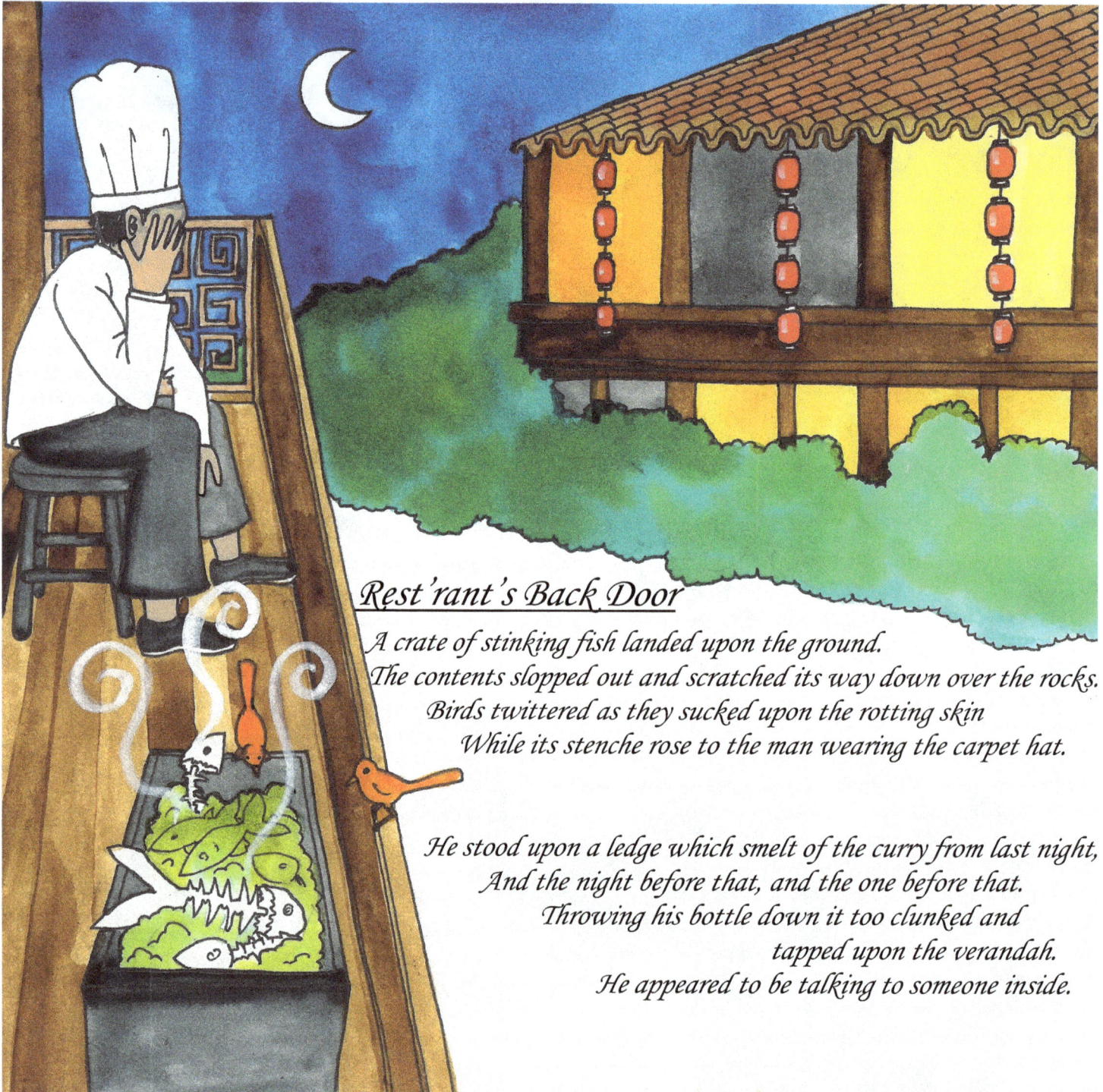

Rest'rant's Back Door

A crate of stinking fish landed upon the ground.
The contents slopped out and scratched its way down over the rocks.
Birds twittered as they sucked upon the rotting skin
While its stenche rose to the man wearing the carpet hat.

He stood upon a ledge which smelt of the curry from last night,
And the night before that, and the one before that.
Throwing his bottle down it too clunked and
tapped upon the verandah.
He appeared to be talking to someone inside.

Watchful Eyes See

Such a thing is not fit for words.
I dare not write of it.
And yet I know that it occurs.
What can be made of this?
Far off, it's said, this evil runs;
They know not it is close
Hidden, even amongst loved ones.
How few see the blatant!
O when will they open their eyes
And their ears hear true words?
O what has happened to the wise?
May good reason be alls.
For the answer is so plain,
It is even, in the eyes.

I Hate Money

I hate money!
I utterly detest it!
It is to me as vomit
Spewn out from an evil mouth
To engulf both north and south.
What has caused more suffering?
Has war? Plague? The noose of sin?
Or even famine ever,
Caused hurt as the coin? Never!

Indeed it is true ~ Money
Is the root of all evil.
But I will never kneel
Before the wicked mammon.
Therefore must I overcome
Earth's ways and spread love to all.
For so few have heard the call
To turn and keep greed at bay

That I may no longer say,
I hate money!

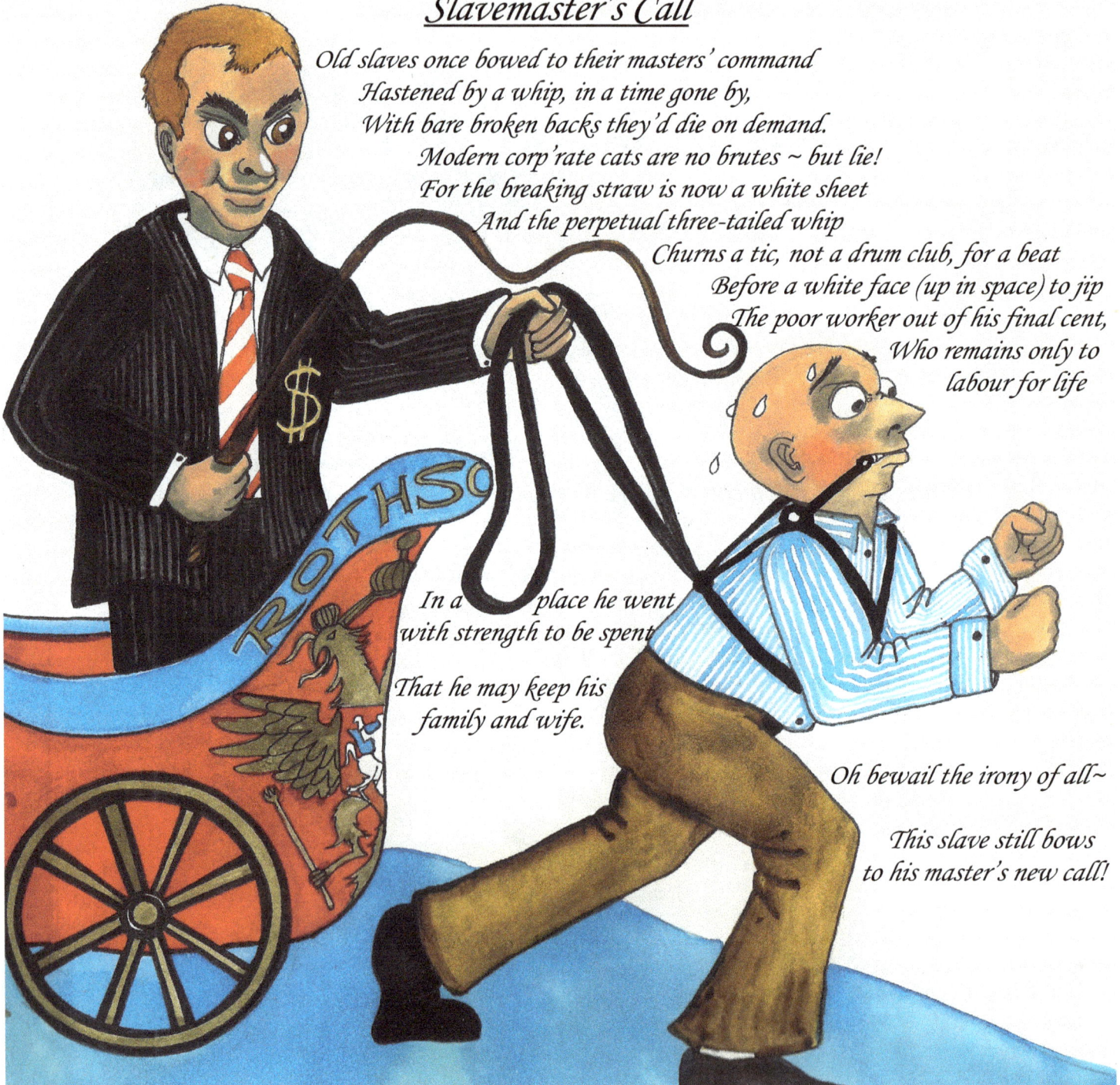

Slavemaster's Call

Old slaves once bowed to their masters' command
Hastened by a whip, in a time gone by,
With bare broken backs they'd die on demand.
Modern corp'rate cats are no brutes ~ but lie!
For the breaking straw is now a white sheet
And the perpetual three-tailed whip

Churns a tic, not a drum club, for a beat
Before a white face (up in space) to jip
The poor worker out of his final cent,
Who remains only to
labour for life

In a   place he went
with strength to be spent

That he may keep his
family and wife.

Oh bewail the irony of all~

This slave still bows
to his master's new call!

No More a Slave

I have a master on earth,
who beats my back with whips.
And another Master in Heaven,
Whose back was whipped sore for me.

I have a master on earth,
who strikes me with hard hands.
And another Master in Heaven,
Who was struck hard in His hands.

I have a master on earth,
who barely lets me eat.
And another Master in Heaven,
Whose Flesh and Blood are my meat.

I have a master without,
and a Master within.
And yet you ask me why I love Him,
and why, it's to Him I cling.

Psalm of Jessy

The Word of the Lord is as cool, sweet,
succulent juice upon my tongue;

It warms as spices and hot curry driving
away the sins of the mouth.

O that the Lord would fill the belly of my
soul with sinless
Bread and Wine from the Vine of Life

And that the Living Water may flow forth
with His Spirit to God's people.

Then would gladness increase greatly on
earth, and many would praise the Lord.

Alleluia.

Old Fashioned Souls

A place where the roads are made for horses
       And the old hardwoods yet still do stand tall,
   Where all the stars survive in their courses
  And dim candlelight shines from the church hall,
 A place untaken by modern forces
And the young love the Valedictine ball,
Where the people's tongue is that of Chaucer's
And coins change hands atop a wooden stall.
In this place our fathers' fathers did live
And we who remain may

remain always,

That we may to friend   and foe good hope give

Until we sleep   at the end of our days.

For in this   dear place old fashioned souls lie

In the hope their hometown may never die.

Passion Arranged

I tell you fellows that now is the time!
Forget set old structures and thought of rhyme.
For upon a whim comes man's emotion
Not in patterns as tides of the ocean.
For some valiant men are men for stealth
And some miserly men are men for wealth.
Some incredible men are men for fame
And some charming men are men for a dame.
But I, I was never as one of these;
For these hear commands and all seek to please.

But to be a man of the word as I
One must forsake earth, declaring,
"Goodbye!"

And set one's
true self,
thoughts and
feelings free,

For the hope of
shared bread,
upon one's knee.

Goodbye Human

Greetings covered creature.
Your message has been received.
As your species is bound for extinction,
We have sent you this gift.
As you are nothing special, you will not be missed.
Thank you for having the courtesy to inform us of your departure.
I feel despondent acceptance.

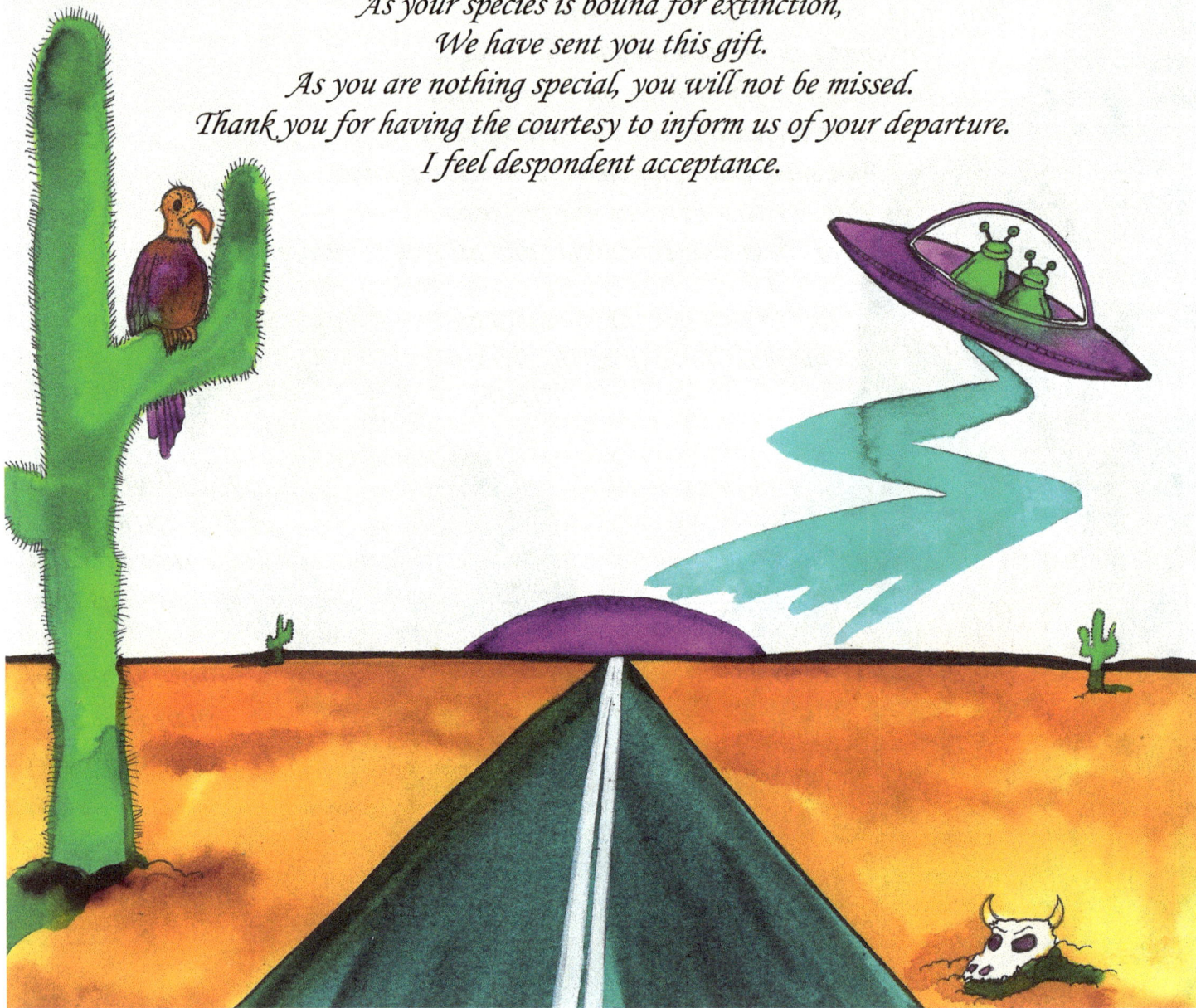

<u>Lost it will Die</u>

Who is this beast that robs us of our language?
Where has he taken the words of English?
How can the poet maintain his flow
When the beast has stolen grammar?
How will we ever describe,
When proud English is lost?
This is now English ~
Nothing, villain!
It's ruined!
Destroyed,
Dead.

About the Author

Jessy is an Australian poet whose uncle has also published a book of poetry. Jessy is popularly known as a Tree as a result of the first poem in this book. In recent years, Jessy has competed in a number of poetry slams, performing a variety of styles.

Jessy has also written a children's book and has plans for a variety of other works including several poetry books and at least one more children's book. However in the future Jessy hopes to produce tales of historical fiction as well.

About the Illustrator

Terri is a freelance illustrator who enjoys the peaceful, undisturbed life of Ireland.

About this Book

This is Jessy Carlisle's premiere poetry book. Originally, it was to be released before Finding Small One but sometimes these sorts of animals get out of the bag before one has a firm hold on them. This selection was chosen to capture an image of some of the wide variety of subjects upon which Jessy has written. Clearly some of the poems are substantially longer than others yet most of these works have been drawn from the poet's shorter creations for the sake of providing an easily digestible literary entrée which may serve as an introduction for readers new to this genre.

Like Jessy Carlisle on Facebook:

www.facebook.com/JessyCarlislePoet

Look out for the following titles also by Jessy Carlisle:

<u>Finding Small One</u>   ***Out Now***

Small One is searching for what's really important in life, but you may be surprised to discover the character's true identity!   (ISBN   9780994179906)

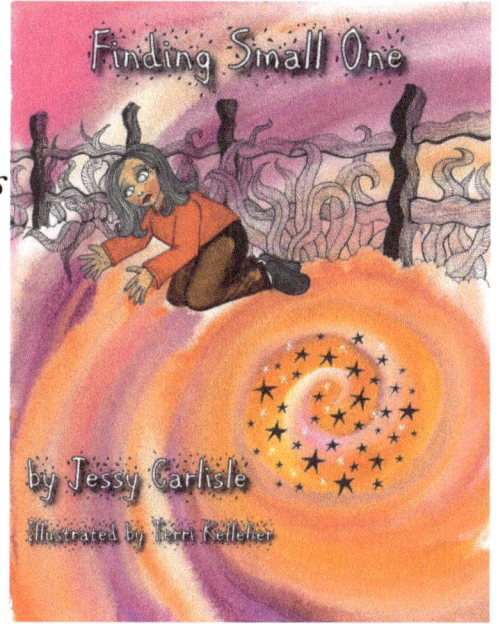

<u>Foolhardy Words</u>   (no release date set)

Some poetical insights upon various life issues plus a little gentle advice.

<u>Ahominem</u>   (no release date set)

A satirical play wherein a divine pantheon debate a most contentious topic.

Jessy Carlisle's poetry may also be found in:

<u>We'll Be Famous When We're Dead</u>   by   Symposium Poetry Society - page 61

<u>Opal Shores : Anthology of Verse</u>   by   Sharon Steward (editor)   - page 44

www.ingramcontent.com/pod-product-compliance
Lightning Source LLC
Chambersburg PA
CBHW062008090426
42811CB00005B/787